COVER LETTER SECRETS

Know what a cover letter is.

In applying for a job, you need to know what a cover letter is so that you would be able to recognize its importance. The cover letter is actually the same as the letter of application, letter of introduction, as well as a transmittal letter. It is a letter that should always accompany the applicant's resume, since not too many employers would consider an application without it.

Read your cover letter several times.

Prior to submitting your cover letter along with your resume, you should read it a good number of times. This is to ensure that you have already indicated all the necessary information in it. Aside from that, it can also help you condition your mind well if you get interviewed.

Do not forget to check for punctuation and grammar.

One of the things that can turn off an employer is when he reads a cover letter that has incorrect grammar and punctuation. Thus, you should not forget checking it for these couple of things. Keep in mind that aside from becoming familiar of the rules in using punctuations, you can also use tools on the web, as well as on your computer, which can help you check on your grammar.

The importance of a cover letter.

In most cases, if you only submit a resume to your potential employer, he would find it useless without the cover letter. The cover letter would let the employer know about the type of work that you can do. Aside from that, it would also let him know how qualified you are for the position that you are applying for.

Keep your letter straight to the point.

Do not use a lot of word fillers when it comes to writing your cover letter. Make sure that it is direct to the point, so that your employer won't have to spend a lot of time in reading it. Keep in mind that aside from reading your cover letter, he also needs to read your resume. Aside from that, he may also have a lot of other cover letters and resumes he needs to check from the other applicants.

Make sure the information in your letter is consistent.

You need to ensure that the information that you indicate in your cover letter is in line with the data you have in your resume. Keep in mind that some statements can become misleading. In other words, it can mean a different thing to the employer from what you are trying to say. Thus, make sure that your statements are clear.

Focus on more important information.

When you write your cover letter, you should be aware of the information that your potential employer is looking for. By doing that, you would have better guidance in writing your cover letter. When you focus on more important information, you would be able to come up with a cover letter that is not too long.

Do your research.

Writing your cover letter should only be done once you have gathered enough information about the position that you are applying for. This would guide you in indicating the data in your cover letter that would be useful for your potential employer. Aside from that, it can also increase your chances in getting interviewed.

Highlight your skills and experiences.

It is necessary to highlight your skills and experiences when you write your cover letter. This is to make the employer realize how qualified you are for the job. Make sure that the experiences and skills you include are related to the position you are applying for, so that they would make sense.

Make sure that you are qualified for the position.

Before deciding to write your cover letter, you need to make sure that you are qualified for the position first. This is to ensure that you won't be wasting your time in composing your cover letter, as well as submitting it to the employer. Check what experiences, talents, and skills the employer is looking for, and see if you have them.

Use the cover letter to explain certain things.

In some cases, there are items in your resume that your potential employer may question. For example, if there are certain gaps in your employment history, then the employer may wonder what happened, or what you were doing during those times when you were out of job. You can take advantage of your cover letter to explain such things.

Your cover letter can serve the same function as your resume's job objective.

Indicating an objective in your resume can make it more specific to the type of job that you really want. Whether you are going to indicate a job objective on it or not, when you write your cover letter, keep in mind that it can serve the same function as your resume's objective. However, the cover letter can be written in a way that you are more open to other job options.

Let your cover letter reflect your personality.

Different individuals have different ways of writing a cover letter. When you write yours, it is best if you can write it in a way that it lets the employer get a glimpse of your own personality. By doing that, it can increase your chances of getting interviewed, especially if the employer realizes that he wants to know you better.

The invited cover letter.

The invited cover letter is when you come up with one in response to a job advertisement. This type of cover letter is not very hard to come up with, since you can base its content in accordance to the job requirements. It is best to make use of this type of cover letter, when you see job advertisements in the newspaper, magazines, and websites.

Pretend that you are the employer.

After writing your cover letter, set it aside for a couple of days, and research more about your potential employer. When you read it again, try to pretend that you are the employer, and see if the letter would be able to impress you. If it can, then it is a sign that you can submit it for the job application soon.

What to do if you can't seem to continue writing your cover letter.

There may be times when you seem to lose focus when it comes to writing up your cover letter. If you are lost for words or you cannot concentrate in trying to finish up your letter, then put a stop to it. You may be under a lot of stress or you simply need a break. Give it a day or two before dealing with it again, so that you can have a fresh start.

Never forget about the benefits that you can derive from the internet.

One of the toughest obstacles you can face in writing a cover letter is getting started with it. To start writing though, you need to have the proper cover letter format. There is no need to worry about it, since you can simply search for cover letter samples on the internet, which can help you out with it.

Put your cover letter and resume side to side.

When it comes to finalizing your resume and cover letter, it is best to put them side to side. By doing that, you can thoroughly check if their formats coincide, as well as their fonts. It is best if they are of the same font, so that they won't look too different from each other. There is no need to match the font size though, but it can also score up more points if they are the same.

The uninvited cover letter.

There are times when you may want to find out if certain companies have job openings or not. When you submit a cover letter in this kind of approach, you would be using the uninvited cover letter type, in which you are presenting yourself to the company and that you are making them aware that they may need someone like you. Even if there are no job opportunities available, submitting this type of cover letter ensures that the company can contact you if they need someone who possesses the skills, talents, and experiences that you have.

You cover letter should be addressed to a specific person.

Starting your cover letter with Dear Sir or Dear Manager is not something that can impress the employer. With that, you have to do your best to find out about the name of the person that you should address it to. By doing that, you are making it more personal, which can score some great points with your employer.

Do not forget to use a good introduction.

The first sentence of your cover letter should be something that can grab the reader's attention. Keep in mind that your employer can be reading hundreds of resumes and cover letters each day. Thus, if you can't grab his attention through your letter's first sentence, then he may not be able to give your letter and your resume a closer look.

Less is more, even with cover letters.

Most employers do not want to read long and boring cover letters and resumes. Therefore, you should make sure that your cover letter has plenty of white spaces after finishing it. Make your cover letter sweet, short, and focused so that you can be called for an interview soon.

Let your employer know what you can do for him.

Do not forget the fact that an employer is looking for someone to hire, in order for that employee to provide something to the company. In other words, you should let him know how the company can benefit in hiring you, so that you can have the chance of being hired. Do your research, and indicate what skills and talents you have that the company can benefit from, so that you would improve your chances.

Choose your words properly.

When it comes to writing your cover letter, there is no need to make use of technical words. Use simple words, since employers do not have time to do research on what certain words may mean. By choosing words and sentences that are easy to understand, your employer would greatly appreciate it, which can make him check your letter and resume further.

It is best to let your potential employer know what action you want him to take after reading your cover letter. For example, it is not a bad idea to indicate that you are looking forward for an interview within the week. By doing this, you can remind the employer that it is the action that he needs to take, if he feels that he should give you a chance.

The referral cover letter.

You may wonder what a referral cover letter is. It is actually a type of cover letter that you can use, especially if you know someone who is a partner or a colleague of your potential employer. In this type of cover letter, you would be indicating the name of the person on the first few sentences of the letter. This is one way to grab the employer's attention, as well as improve your chances against your competition.

Sleep well before writing your cover letter.

Always remember that your cover letter is one of the factors that can determine your chances in landing on the job that you really want. With that, you need to ensure that you have the right mindset in writing it. One of the ways that can help you achieve that is to get some sleep just before writing it. Thus, if you are writing it at night, then get a 15 minute nap first, so that you can feel refreshed afterwards.

Be patient.

There may be times when writing a cover letter for a specific job vacancy is tough. You need to be patient with it, so that you won't end up throwing lots of papers into the garbage bin. If you are getting overwhelmed, take a deep breath and close your eyes, before pursuing it again.

Let your friend read it.

Having a friend or a close family member read your cover letter is not a bad idea. By doing this, you can ensure that your cover letter sounds really good. Aside from that, the reader can also give you some tips in improving it, if it really needs to be modified.

Check out cover letter samples.

There are lots of cover letter samples that you can read through the internet these days. Prior to starting on your own letter, it is a good idea to check out these samples first. When you check them, it would give you a better idea on how to get started on it. Aside from that, it can also provide you guidance in following the right format for it.

Do not submit a generic cover letter.

Always remember that employers are used to reading thousands of cover letters. In other words, in most cases, they would immediately notice it if the cover letter they are reading is one of the mass produced copies. Generic cover letters usually do not give that much impression on the employers. Thus, you need to make sure that you write an original cover letter for every job position that you are applying for, so that you can have a better chance of being employed.

Do not forget to indicate your contact information.

It is necessary to include your contact information on your cover letter, since it would be the only way for the employer to call you for an interview. You need to make sure that you also indicate an alternate number, in case the primary one is not available. Aside from that, you should also ensure that the numbers you have provided are directed towards you and not through other people or answering machines.

Make sure that your cover letter is easy to read.

Enhancing your cover letter's reader-friendliness is necessary, so that your potential employer would be able to read it well. To achieve that, you can actually make use of bullets and other special formatting techniques. Aside from making it reader-friendly, you should also make it as short as possible.

Sign your cover letter with your name.

One of the worst things that you can do in coming up with a cover letter is submitting it without your name and signature. Signing the cover letter is one of the ways that you can show that you are truthful and committed to the statements that you have mentioned. When it comes to signing the letter though, make sure that you sign it boldly, since it indicates confidence.

Make sure that the tone of the letter is just right.

It is important that your cover letter has a tone that indicates your self-confidence. However, you should not overdo it, since it can also sound arrogant. To check if it has the right tone, you should try to read it again and again, and imagine that you are not the one who has written it. Aside from that, you should also ask your honest friend to read it for you.

Make your letter interesting.

If you are the employer, one of the things that may stop you from reading a cover letter is if its boring. Thus, you should make sure that yours is not boring, and it should be interesting. Focus on interesting statements and enthusiastic words, so that your employer would want to read it from top to bottom.

Be aware of the common mistakes of generic cover letters.

When you have a generic form of a cover letter, in most cases, you only need to edit certain details to it, such as the date, the name that you are addressing it to, and such. However, this is actually one of the things that can make you commit a mistake in submitting it. If you forget to change these details, then you cannot expect your potential employer to call you for an interview. Thus, you should refrain from using these types of cover letters, so that you can prevent such mistakes to happen.

A cover letter that is a response for an advertisement.

If you are writing a cover letter in response for a job advertisement, then you should make sure that you are mindful of the requirements of the position. This way, you can indicate your skills, talents, and experiences on your cover letter, which satisfy the requirements. When you do this, it would become easier for the reader to tell if you are qualified or not.

Do not forget about your transferable skills.

Transferable skills are those that you have learned or acquired in different activities in your life. Some examples of these activities would be parenting, jobs, projects, classes, sports, and many more. When you talk about them in your cover letter, it can improve your chances of getting hired, since they are transferable and can be applied in whatever types of jobs you want to do.

Keep your cover letter conversational.

When you keep your cover letter as conversational as possible, you are showing some personality to the reader. Thus, it would lessen the chances that he would skip reading it entirely. Aside from that, it would also convince him that you know how to build rapport, even when you have not met yet.

Don't forget about your achievements.

An employer knows that when they hire a new employee, they have to spend time and money in developing him, as well as in paying for his services. Thus, they want the best in the field. With that, you should not forget to tell them about your achievements through your cover letter, so that they would know your potentials.

Indicating that you are willing to learn.

When you write that you are willing to learn, you have to consider that it can mean different things to different employers. It can mean that you are open to other functions in the job. However, it can also remind the employer about training as well as expenses. Thus, it should be safer if you would not be including this statement in your letter. Focus more on what you can contribute to the company, since that is the main factor that your employer would be checking out.

Do not forget to indicate your abilities to meet deadlines.

One of the concerns employers have when it comes to hiring a new employee is whether the new worker can meet deadlines. This is because, this part of the job is very important, since it is a factor that can affect the overall performance of the business. Thus, you have to let them know that you have this ability, so that they would be assured that hiring you would be a chance that they are willing to take.

Never parrot your resume.

There is no use for a cover letter if you are just going to parrot your resume with it. This is because, your employer would realize that he has just wasted his time in reading both documents. Thus, the cover letter should not just parrot the resume. It should elaborate your resume and explain certain things about it.

Do not sound weak when you send out a cover letter through email.

When you submit a cover letter through email, you should not tell your employer that your resume is attached for them to read it if they want to. This is telling them that you are not even sure if your resume is worth reading. Say something direct, and expect them to read it, so that they would do so.

Listing hobbies and interests.

It is a common practice for some to list down hobbies and interests into their cover letters. However, before listing them down, you should think whether they are really relevant to the position or not. If you are unsure, then it is safer not to include them, so that you won't make your cover letter longer than it should be.

You can refer them to your previous employer if you want to.

In writing your cover letter, you would want to sell yourself to your potential employer by making value judgments about yourself. To add more credibility in them though, you can always refer them to your previous employer or tell them that your previous employer can attest to it. By doing this, they would not even bother calling your employer about it, and would just take your word for it.

Don't forget your ability to handle multiple tasks.

Handling multiple tasks is a skill that you may have acquired from an unrelated field of work. However, you can use it on your cover letter, since you can apply it to any kind of work. Do not forget to mention is, since lots of employers want their workers to handle multiple tasks. It is a benefit that you can offer to them, which would increase your chances of getting hired.

Being dynamic.

Lots of companies today go through constant change, whether in the kind of operations that they do, or by dealing with their customers. Thus, it is a good idea to tell them that you are dynamic. This means that you are flexible, and that they can depend on you when changes have to be made.

The opening paragraph of your cover letter.

The opening paragraph of your cover letter should be written in a way that it grabs the attention of the reader. This is where you can state what your intentions are. Aside from that, this is also the paragraph where you can let them have an idea about what you can do for them.

The number of paragraphs you should have in the cover letter.

In the cover letter, having three paragraphs in it should be good enough. If you need to elaborate more though, having four paragraphs is not bad. Each of the paragraphs in the cover letter should have different content, and there should be about three or four sentences in it.

Formatting your cover letter.

Leaving plenty of spaces or white spaces in your cover letter is a good idea. Thus, when you format your cover letter, it is a good idea to have generous margins in it. Aside from that, using double space between paragraphs should also be a good step to take.

Number of pages in the cover letter.

Always remember that your potential employer may have to go through reading fifty to a hundred cover letters and resumes in a day. In other words, it is quite a tedious task for him. With that, if you are wondering about the number of pages you should have for your cover letter, then you should only keep it to one. There are no exceptions for it, since it is best if your cover letter is short and easy to understand.

Check for spelling mistakes.

There is always a chance for you to misspell certain words, especially if you have prepared a cover letter in just a short amount of time. Thus, you should thoroughly check it for spelling errors. To do that, you can read your cover letter a lot of times,. Aside from that, you can also make use of some tools for it.

Express your long term interest in the job your are applying for.

In preparing your cover letter, you need to let your potential employer get the idea that you are interested in working for him for a long term engagement. Keep in mind that most employers do not want to go through a hiring process all the time. Thus, if you can subtly express your long term interest, then you would be able to improve your chances for it.

Never complain about your previous employer in your cover letter.

It is never a good idea to complain about your previous employer either in your cover letter or in your job interview. This is because, your potential employer would think that you can also do the same thing, if you decide to leave them. Focus on writing positive statements in your cover letter, so that the reader would have a more pleasant time in going through it.

Your cover letter and your resume has different purposes.

When you are in the process of writing your cover letter, you should always keep in mind that it has a different purpose as your resume. In other words, even if you want to make it in a way that it is related to your resume, you should not depend on your resume to do the work in convincing the employer to give you a chance. Your cover letter is your chance to elaborate on your qualifications and skills, which would become the reasons why you are fit for the job.

What happens when you express negative things in your cover letter.

Expressing negative things in your cover letter, such as complaining about your previous jobs, can jeopardize your chances in getting the job you want. This is because it can make your potential employer think that you are ungrateful, unappreciative, and disloyal. Aside from that, it can also make him realize that he does not want you on his team.

Attention grabbing statements.

At the first paragraph of your cover letter, you should make use of attention grabbing statements. However, you should not use such statements just for the sake of grabbing the attention of your reader. The statements should be relevant to the job that you are applying for, so that the person reading it would be captivated.

Focus on your strengths.

Cover letters should express your strengths, instead of your weaknesses. It should not make its reader picture you as someone who is desperate, needy, and weak. Position yourself as an excellent choice for your potential employer by focusing on your strengths, so that you would make him believe that you should be given a chance.

Do not make a cover letter for a job that does not match your experiences and skills.

It may be true that you won't lose anything in submitting a cover letter and a resume for a job that does not match your experiences and skills. However, you would actually be wasting your time in it. Aside from that, you would also be wasting other people's time as well.

Tailor-fit your cover letter to the job you are applying for.

Although it is helpful if you have a basic format that you can follow in writing a cover letter, it is still best if you tailor-fit it to the job that you are applying for. Doing this would make your cover letter appear more original. Aside from that, it would also increase your chances of getting interviewed, since employers do not like generic letters.

Minimize the number of words.

When you write your cover letter, you should minimize the number of words that you include in it. When you think about this while coming up with the letter, you would be able to have a cover letter that is precise and direct to the point. Aside from that, it would also help you in making the whole letter short and easy to comprehend.

You can give examples.

When it comes to proving your claims in your cover letter, such as going the extra mile in serving a customer, you can always site examples for it. Just make sure that the example is written in just a short paragraph. In doing this, you are amplifying your desirable trait, which would make your reader remember you more.

Become a sales person.

Think of yourself as a sales person when you are writing your cover letter. Think about it as your sales letter, in which you need to convince someone to buy a product. The product here is you, and if you focus on the benefits that they can enjoy in hiring you, then you can increase your chances of being selected.

Use action words.

Writing a cover letter should involve the use of action words. This is because, you want it to be active instead of passive. When you make use of action words, the letter's reader would be able to picture out what you are trying to say better. Aside from that, it can also help them decide in what they need to do next, after reading it.

Leave the ball in your potential employer's court.

In writing and submitting your cover letter, think of it as your action, in which your reader would have to react to. With that, you should come up with a letter that has a call to action. In other words, before ending it, state that you are requesting for an interview. Aside from that, you can also be proactive and state that you are going to make a follow up by giving them a call.

The best type of cover letter.

In general, there are three types of cover letters. They are the invited, uninvited, and the referral cover letter. It is best to become more familiar of the different purpose each of the different cover letters has. When you do that, you would be able to identify the best type of cover letter for your situation.

Your unique selling proposition.

Some people have no clue about the most important thing that they have to include in the cover letter. It is actually your unique selling proposition. This is where you need to let your potential employer know why you are a better choice for them to make, than the other applicants for the job.

Imagine what your employer is thinking.

In order to have a very effective cover letter, you should imagine what the reader is thinking when you are writing it. In most cases, your employer would be thinking about why he should be hiring you. Thus, make sure that your letter provides him the reasons to hire you, so that he would do so.
Make your cover letter unique.

If you are going to check on samples of cover letters online, you would find out that most of them would follow basic letter formats. In other words, there would just be 3 or 4 paragraphs in it and such. To make it more unique, you can actually highlight your qualifications or bold them. You can also identify your skills with bullets if you want to. When you do that, the reader would be glad to have something that is different, and it would actually make your letter easier to read.

Including references in the cover letter.

There is no need to indicate your references in the cover letter. You only need to indicate them if it is required by the employer. In most cases though, you only need to provide your references when you have already gone through interviews, and that you are at the end stages of the hiring process.

Ask your friends for help.

Having a lot of friends would definitely help you in coming up with an excellent cover letter. If you have a friend who is a member of the hiring department of a company, then you can ask him for help in evaluating your cover letter. Let him read your cover letter and make adjustments if they are needed before submitting it.

Get to the point in writing your letter.

Writing a cover letter that is effective can be done by getting directly to the point. When you beat around the bush, your potential employer would be tired in reading your lengthy cover letter. This can make him lose interest in your qualifications and skills, which can hinder your chances of getting hired.

Using challenging thoughts.

A cover letter with challenging thoughts can increase your chances of getting interviewed by your potential employer. This is because, it can get them convinced that talking to you is worthwhile. Aside from that, it can even make them contact you for an interview, even when they are not planning to hire anyone today.

Compliment the company.

If the company that you are applying for has achieved something recently, then you should take note of it. This is because, you can make use of that in your cover letter. Complimenting your potential employer about his company's recent achievement is a good attention grabber. Thus, you can use it in your opening paragraph, so that the reader would be motivated in reading the entire letter.

Don't hesitate to reconstruct your cover letter.

If your friend has told you that your cover letter needs modifications, and you are convinced that he is correct, then you should not hesitate in doing it all over again. Keep in mind that your cover letter needs to be perfect so that you can land on an interview. With that, it is best to write it as early as possible, so that you won't be rushing yourself.

Your cover letter's second paragraph.

A good cover letter has to have about 3 to 4 short paragraphs in it. While the first paragraph focuses on getting the attention of the reader, the second should be all about your professional and academic qualifications. This is where you get to provide supplemental information about how the company can benefit in hiring you.

You should not sound too presumptuous in your first paragraph.

If you become too presumptuous in your first paragraph, your reader may feel that you are trying to tell him what he needs to do next. This is actually not a good idea, since your employer may resent it. Thus, make sure that you don't have any statements in your letter that is too presumptuous, so that your chances in getting hired would be good.

There is no need to discuss too many things in the cover letter.

Although the cover letter is usually the first thing that an employer would read, there is no need to discuss so much things in it. This is because, it is better if your letter is brief. However, do not put too much limitations on it. Make sure that you can elaborate your skills and qualifications in it, which you cannot do in your resume, so that your employer can see the reasons why they should consider you for the position.

Always think positive.

Even if it is going to be your first time to write a cover letter, you should still think positive about it. In other words, you should believe that you can come up with something that is effective. When you become more positive about it, then you can also come up with a letter that can convince your employer to contact you for an interview.

What to focus on when you do not have the necessary job experience yet.

There are times when you may lose confidence in writing your cover letter for the reason that you don't have the experiences, which can boost your qualifications for the job. When you are in this situation, you should try to focus more on your transferable skills. This is because, such types of skills can be done in different fields, and if your employer can see that, then he may be convinced to discuss your qualifications in person.

Writing the third paragraph of the cover letter.

If your first paragraph is all about getting the attention of the reader, and your second one has discussed your skills and qualifications, then you should also know what to indicate in your third paragraph. In your third paragraph, you can actually continue discussing your qualifications, but relate yourself to the company as well. This is where you can also show your knowledge about the company.

Be confident.

If you lack self-confidence, then you may not be able to come up with a cover letter that can convince your reader to hire you. Thus, you need to build up your confidence first. Try to recall how you were able to help out your previous employers, so that you can remind yourself about how good you have contributed to them. Aside from that, you should also not forget about your educational attainments.

Accentuate the positive in your cover letters.

Using phrases such as I Believe and I Feel is something that is not strong enough to accentuate the positive in your cover letters. In other words, they can make your cover letter weak, which can reflect the lack of confidence. Instead of using such phrases, replace them with I Am Positive or I Am Convinced.

State the time that you are available in your cover letter.

It is in your final paragraph that you should show your interest in getting interviewed. However, you should be specific about the time that you are available. In other words, you should not forget to indicate the days of the week that you are available, as well as the times.

Cover letter template.

If you don't have an idea on how to write a cover letter, then you can always make use of a template for that. There are lots of cover letter samples that you can find on the internet today. You can actually make use of some of them as your templates, so that you would be guided in getting started with your letter.

Sending a cover letter through email.

If you want to send a cover letter through email, then you should do it by making it as an attachment. This is because, reading a cover letter through an actual email is actually not good, especially when it comes to formatting it. When you send it as an attachment, not only would the reader be able to go through it easily, but he can also print it with ease if he wants to.

Do not forget to explain your employment gap.

When you submit your resume, which comes with your employment record, it may be possible that your potential employer would wonder about the dates when you were not employed. With that, you should

take advantage of the cover letter to explain it. Do it briefly on the second or third paragraph, and immediately revert back your reader's attention to your achievements and qualifications.

Show how enthusiastic you are the end of the letter.

Before you end the letter, you should express your enthusiasm about getting interviewed by the employer. Say how excited you are in meeting them. When you do that, your potential employer would be convinced that you are indeed very interested in the position that you are applying for.

Take time in making your cover letter.

Keep in mind that writing a cover letter is something that can take time, especially if you are serious about it. Thus, you should not rush yourself in doing it. Aside from that, review your letter for a good number of times, so that you can ensure that it would increase your chances of getting interviewed for the job.

Use words that show your passion and enthusiasm.

Enthusiasm and passion are two important factors that employers want their potential employees to have. This is because, it reflects the motivation of the individual when it comes to his work. Thus, when you write your cover letter, you should use words that can express your passion and enthusiasm for the job that you are applying for.

Necessary parts in the cover letter.

To come up with a complete and effective cover letter, you should know the parts or sections that need to be included in it. These are the salutation, the data that explains why you are to be given a chance for the job, closing, your signature, as well as the contact section. By focusing on these parts, it would help you start writing your letter and prevent you from forgetting information that needs to be included in it.

How to come up with a targeted cover letter.

A targeted cover letter means that you are making it to target the job that you want. To achieve that, you have to list the criteria that the employer has for the job opening. After which, you should also list down all your skills and experiences. By doing that, you should be able to identify your skills and experiences, which would perfectly fit the criteria of the employer, and include only them in your cover letter.

Reasons to customize your cover letter.

It is true that it can be time consuming to customize your cover letter to every job that you are applying for. However, it would actually increase your chances of getting hired when you do it. When you customize your letter, it would show your employer why you and the company are a perfect match.

Emailing cover letters.

In most cases, if you are sending a cover letter through email, there are specific instructions provided by your potential employer. With that, you need to make sure that you follow it to the letter, so that your application would be considered. Thus, if he wants you to copy and past the letter to the email body on top of attaching it, then you should follow it. Aside from that, it is also possible that he requires specific font and font size for it.

Hiring someone to make your cover letter.

There may be people today who may offer their services in writing cover letters. Although they offer utmost convenience, hiring one may not increase your chances in getting hired. This is because, when someone else has written your cover letter, then you may not be very familiar about it. Aside from that, it would also lack your personal touch.

Learning more about how to make a cover letter.

If you want to learn more about how to be effective in writing a cover letter, you can always do your research about it online. Aside from the fact that there are lots of websites that offer cover letter samples, there are also online tutorials that are offered for free. Do your research online, so that it would be very convenient for you.

There is no need to reveal every detail of your background.

Keep in mind that there is no need to reveal every detail of your background in your cover letter. This is because, when you do this, you may accidentally reveal certain weaknesses that you have without intending to. Always remember that it is best to always focus on your strengths; thus, do not dig in too deep into your past to avoid revealing your weaknesses.

Write more cover letters.

To gain more experience in writing cover letters, you should write more. Thus, if there are lots of job vacancies that you can apply for, then start coming up with personalized cover letters today. The more cover letters you are able to write, the more you would become comfortable in it.

www.ingramcontent.com/pod-product-compliance
Lightning Source LLC
Chambersburg PA
CBHW071204220526
45468CB00003B/1153